UNTETHERED GROUNDS

A Collection of Poems

BILLIE BIOKU

ARCHWAY
PUBLISHING

Archway Publishing books may be ordered
through booksellers or by contacting:

Archway Publishing
1663 Liberty Drive
Bloomington, IN 47403
www.archwaypublishing.com
844-669-3957

ISBN: 978-1-6657-4312-9 (sc)
ISBN: 978-1-6657-4313-6 (hc)
ISBN: 978-1-6657-4314-3 (e)

Library of Congress Control Number: 2023908099

Print information available on the last page.

Archway Publishing rev. date: 04/26/2023

"Discovery is seeing what everybody else has seen and thinking what nobody else has thought."
-Dr. Albert Szent-Gyorgyi

Contents

1) Grounded in the Elements

Rowing Water 2

- Wandering Child 3
- Precipitation 4
- Fountain Breach 5
- August 6
- Wingspan 7
- Frothy Water..8
- Morning Dew 9

Fervid Fire..10

- Eternal Flame 11
- Heated Desires 12
- Perfect Match 13
- Apocalypse 14
- Burnt Foundation 15
- Solid Ground..16
- California 17

Rocky Earth...18

- Mojave Desert...19
- Normandy 20
- The Unforgettable Hike 21
- Forest Moments..22
- Touched Grass..23
- Communal Grounds 24
- Montecito 25

Crisp Air..27

- Summer Days..28
- Deep Breaths 29

- Wind Lifts 30
- Silver Moon 31
- The Ecosystem 32
- Airplanes 33
- Spiked-Stars 34

2) Grounded in Society

Suffering & Smiling 36

- Grinds & Flows 37
- Struggles We Face 38
- Realisms 39
- Competition.................................. 40
- Still Looking, Still Dreaming...................... 41
- Grit 43
- Newfound Changes 44

Familial Connections 45

- Hearty Questions.......................... 46
- The Figurine................................. 47
- Breaking Free 48
- The Never-ending Race 49
- Character Built 50
- Friend to Myself........................... 51
- Rooted... 52

3) Grounded in Self

Body Inhibitions 54

- Fluticasone Lungs......................... 55
- Aching Arthritis............................ 57
- Purging 58
- Dysmorphic Tales 59
- Hives 60

- Areata 61
- Gaping Black Hole 62

4) Grounded in Humanity

City Life? 64

- Peoplehood 65
- Print + Digital Culture 67
- Snapshot Friendship 68
- Sense of Fear 70
- Identity 71
- Untold Story 73
- Cultivated Crisis 74

Economic Restorations 76

- Hand Ups 77
- Global Phenomenon 79
- The Nethermost Billion 80
- Sink and Swim 82
- The Agreement 83
- Free-Rider 85
- Developed Leadership 86

Lessons Learned 87

- The Neighbor 88
- Forgiven Freedom 90
- Opaque Findings 92
- Blind Spots 94
- The Eyes 96
- Shapeable Perseverance 98
- Clothed in Love 100

SECTION 1

Grounded in the Elements

Rowing Water

Wandering Child

I enter the pristine cave located at the edge of the coastline.

Beneath the surface lies underwater aliens.

With one touch, lightning bolts of shock waves flow through the body.

Urine is needed to mollify the sting.

The wild rivers create a ripple effect.

I tend to dip my feet into the concoction.

Composite elements form a hybrid breed.

The peonies whir and tumble exquisitely.

I can hear a storm coming from ashore.

To home, I return.

Precipitation

Rain pours over the sea.

Tiny drops touch the outer-layer skin of the mammals.

They relish in the sound of protection.

Heavy falls shower onto the forest trees.

It's neither a mizzle nor a drizzle.

Misty air lets out a gooey dew.

The foggy cloud has reached the surface of the universe.

Ground touched.

It's hard to see through anything; my vision has been obscured.

Gray clouds conceal the beauty of the sun.

A glimmer of hope is what I hold onto.

Fountain Breach

I want to go back in time to enjoy my youth again.

Translucent lakes, can you see the light?

The fountain is so high; I struggle to climb up the mountain.

The key to true happiness lies somewhere over there.

Misconceived notions, I have a strange feeling.

I once dreamt of an alcove where all my dreams would come true.

I open my eyes to unravel the vessels of the unknown.

The cryptic cipher quivers and shakes.

The writing cannot yet be unlocked.

August

We like to relax by the pool.

Clasped hands, we are open to new possibilities.

Our feet swing swiftly above the water.

We begin to discover the heart of this land.

Drowning our fears in the cold serene chlorine.

We're swallowed whole and dry.

Signs ignored; we dive into the unfamiliar liquid.

Our names written inside of history books.

We're kept from sinking to the bottom.

Sea horses gallop to the waning crescent moon.

A new phase has begun.

Wingspan

I sometimes sing a tune to the sea.

It happens when I'm feeling deeply blue.

The mammals happily squeal to the sound of my voice.

I finally feel as though I belong.

Whales create splashes by the harbor.

But the Albatross birds are still suffering.

Plastic consumes their intestines; they struggle to feed their offspring.

There's not enough zooplankton for this keystone species.

They live and breathe water; it's all that they know.

Southern hemisphere is home to these soaring feathered friends.

Haven't we traveled far enough?

Clearer skies for a brighter tomorrow.

Frothy Water

There's a turbulent reaction; a break in the magnetic pull.

Rapid flows of water, it's a chain reaction.

Collapse into the cords we seek to escape.

Your scars sparkle when the sun wakes up.

It's my favorite part.

You drift out to sea as the water rises.

Swirling around at the sound of thunder.

Miles away from home.

You go swimming with the wildly hunted in Faroe Islands.

Unbeknownst to me, you let go.

Waves break at the undertow.

Still, your head remains above water.

Morning Dew

I looked for you out in the fields, but you were nowhere to be found.

Your soul left to go skipping in the balanced ocean.

I fixed my eyes on the rustling leaves.

Green veins, your blood is blue.

Turbulent quiet minds let out a slow whisper.

Reckless love, I gently hold on to the flower's stem.

I watch as the ship's wheels turn against the seabed.

You went out to sea to save it.

Locked doors have no hold on your strength.

Open windows, rescue mission complete.

The argent snow falls gracefully into the water.

Hurry up my love, winter is near!

Fervid Fire

Eternal Flame

There seems to be an incessant flow of steam.

The fumes are coming from inside the superior vena cava.

An obstruction of blood flow has taken place.

Deoxygenation—it has become difficult to breathe.

Can't you see that I'm burning for your love?

Engulfed in the promises you tell me.

You place your hand on my heart and listen patiently to its beats.

I place my hand on your heart and can feel the same beat.

The rhythm matches oh so perfectly.

Souls tied together by the eternal flame.

Our love knows no bounds, it can light up the world.

Desires quenched by the imposition of tender longings.

Heated Desires

Did someone turn up the temperature?

It has risen so quickly.

My cheeks have turned a pinkish red.

I am overwhelmed with emotion.

I can't place my finger on it yet.

Suddenly, I can feel a warm gust of air breathing heavily down on my neck.

You.

The hottest man I know has arrived back in town.

Oh, won't you light up my fire?

My smokey eyeliner has smeared across my face.

Tears of sadness quickly burned away.

Misty eyes remain.

There's no hesitation in the decisions we make.

Perfect Match

I feel lighter now that he's no longer in my life anymore.

I had to let go of him to realize what I truly needed.

You stepped into my life at the right moment.

You helped to ignite my truest desires.

Our love is both passionate and pure.

Devotion floods through the chambers of my heart.

My brain burns with knowledge, I come to know your neurons deeply.

Twists and turns throughout; our kisses have become flammable.

Ice cubes slip down our skin to help cool down the hot sun's effect.

Fire it up—I'm ready for more!

Apocalypse

The chimney is filled with smoke.

From the mountain side, we can see the desolated fire.

Startled goats, leopards, and sheep run away feeling petrified.

We must pack our bags and quickly go.

Confined to our surroundings, there is nowhere to turn.

Trees are burning nearby—the fire's making its way to our home.

From the ajar door, we can hear people screaming.

There's not enough breeze to stop the pain.

It's already hard to breathe in here; the masks aren't working.

The hot springs around the corner have begun to boil.

It feels like we're in an apocalypse.

Burnt Foundation

Skyscrapers crumble back down to its elements.

Men in uniform rush to spray water on the burning building.

Footprints land on the dusty ground.

Forming patterns from the lining of the shoe.

Cemented into the ground, the fuel leaves a sticky path.

Residue from the heat extinguishes away.

Oxygen starts up a chemical reaction.

Rain comes pouring down to caress the fire.

The people are left with nothing.

Some cry out and mourn in agony.

Others rejoice for they believe it's the start of something new.

Solid Ground

Enmeshed twigs struck by lightning.

On accident, a wildfire has been created.

On purpose, farmers use controlled fires to manage their land.

Smoke pollutes from the natural vegetation.

The air feels stuffy and dry.

Greenhouse gases released to degrade our ecosystem.

Plants wait patiently for a blaze to reproduce.

Winds rapidly move to intensify the spread.

The fire planet strikes again!

California

It's on fire, yet again.

Endorphins block out the pain we feel inside.

Looks like it is time to move again.

Wildfires are set free, but somehow, we feel stuck.

The sunsets and stars make the discomfort bearable.

We're surrounded by burning palm trees.

The pamphlets were wrong.

It still gets gloomy in California.

Glossed over imperfections, where is the reality?

Energetic people feel empty inside.

Someday we'll be left with nothing but our ashes.

Rocky Earth

Rocky Earth

Mojave Desert

We made our way through the Joshua Trees.

The rust-colored dust from the ground crept onto my skin.

I saw a bug-eyed cicada and started to run.

I haven't seen one since I was a young child in Maryland.

You chortled at my misery, and said to me "honeybee, they don't bite."

We watched as the snow fell gracefully onto the broccoli-shaped florets.

Here in the hidden valley, everything becomes known.

Memories untold, it started to get cold.

We wrapped ourselves around the Mexican blanket.

Stories shared, tomorrow we'll search for the wildflowers.

Normandy

I left my chateau late at night in search of an adventure.

I wanted to explore the countryside at dusk.

Streetlights gone missing; I couldn't see a thing.

Senses heightened; fear grew inside of me.

Loud growls from nearby grew closer and closer.

I was warned earlier that bison lived across the street.

I was forewarned of the dangers of going out alone at night.

But why didn't I listen?

The bison were now chasing after me.

Fight or flight.

I started to run.

My legs became tired, but I could not stop.

Now parallel to me, I began to sprint.

Dirt at the bottom of my shoes, I did not care.

Back to safety, what a relief!

Story retold: The host smirked and said to me, "Told you so!"

The Unforgettable Hike

We went hiking on the San Ysidro Trail.

I soaked in all the beauty of the wilderness.

Steep incline: this trail had its way with me.

Running shoes on a hike meant disaster would soon strike.

I slipped on a rock at the edge of a cliff.

My friends quickly grabbed my arm to stop me from falling.

Miracles I sometimes take for granted.

As we continued the hike, I saw an astonishing monarch butterfly.

Mesmerized by its beauty, I guilelessly stared.

But we had to trudge forward to the creek.

Finally, we arrived at our destination.

Before us was a lofty cascading waterfall.

Sighted splendid rainbows made the experience worthwhile.

Sometimes the end justifies the means.

Forest Moments

In the wilderness, I am fully known.

The branches of the trees leave scratches on my legs.

I like to wander around and listen to different creatures making sounds.

I wonder about what it would be like to take camp in the woods.

For more than awhile.

Where the trees meet the water across from the mountains.

Loveliness undisturbed by human development.

Filtration of the healthy ecosystem.

Resplendent leaves fall as the season starts to change.

We strive to live in harmony with nature.

Touched Grass

The flowers bloom to signify the start of spring.

We are happy-hearted.

Overripe fruit produce organic sweet sugar on my tongue.

We take a road trip without a map in hand.

The open road is our great playground.

Chasing dreams is what we know best to do.

This weather is so dreamy, we must take a couple of naps.

We fall asleep on a cliff that overlooks the ocean.

You pluck a daisy from the ground and place it in my hair.

We blast the music from the radio and dance cheerfully in the middle of the street.

Sometimes it's nice to take a break from the real world.

Communal Grounds

Walks around the boulevard; the streets are empty.

Echoes in the pavement, our recollections start to fade.

Out in the open, the Northern Lights are only visible to some.

In the city, I am surrounded but still feel alone.

But we all long for something.

Fixated on sights we try to understand.

Down by the water it is peaceful but also lonely.

In communities we prosper and thrive.

Alpine habitats, I am trying to find my grounding.

Rocky Earth

Montecito

After the fire, we thought that we were safe.

Our soil was strong enough to withstand anything.

But we were wrong.

Topsoil tarnished by the blaze.

The air still stifled with smoke.

Roots once planted would soon disappear.

To our dismay, the worse had yet to come.

Rain came pouring down heavily, we weren't used to it.

Years of a drought, the ground decided to sing a different tune.

Unpaved seasons, this rainfall would be different.

Some slept peacefully to the sound of water touching the ground.

Others fought avidly with the chaos.

Awoken to the horrific news, we couldn't believe our ears.

Mudslides.

Debris flows blocked pathways.

Rocky Earth

Homes destroyed by the piling of boulders.

Swept away into the weeping ocean.

Lives forever changed; it was a battle cry.

Flood's occurrence led to an unfathomable destruction.

God, please provide comfort and healing to those still hurting.

Crisp Air

Summary Days

I took a stroll through the park.

The summer wind breezed through my hair.

Children cheered along as their kites flew in the air.

Birds chirped and twirled in the sky.

The flowers gleefully swayed back and forth.

The smell of fresh pasta lingered around.

I ate an almond croissant that had a sweet gooey consistency to it.

Dogs playfully tussled as they tried to catch the tossed stick.

After a hard day of work, this was much needed.

Deep Breaths

The winds are changing.

But you remain the same.

You simply take my breath away.

Air blown onto my skin.

Goosebumps get created.

This moment is magical.

Distant memories come to the present.

Consciously aware of all our wants.

Brighter futures made from the decisions of today.

We inhale each other's bodily chemicals; Exhale away the toxicity.

In ourselves we our found again.

Wind Lifts

One night as I was walking home, the wind was very robust.

I could feel my feet being lifted from the ground.

I fought hard and long against the current.

But it was too powerful.

I was overcome by its astounding strength.

So, I gave up and let it have its way with me.

I drifted throughout the streets until I could find a tree to hold onto.

As the wind came to a halt, I took cover behind the tree.

Small pieces of rock flung at me.

I braced for impact, but it flew past me.

Dodging the rocks as best as I could, I was finally safe.

I silently walked back home and told no one of my experience.

Silver Moon

The sky is clear to reveal a jaw-dropping sight.

A white glow casted onto the water.

The moon has made its presence known.

I take out a telescope to observe it more closely.

Its craters are crafted to perfection.

From dusk till dawn, it makes its mark on the Earth.

I see my reflection in the snow-covered satellite.

The moonlight provides protection when the streetlights forget to.

In the wee hours of the morning, I watch as it fades away.

Moonshine in hand, I kick back and relax.

The eased mind I have brings peace to the moon.

The Ecosystem

Wind carries away germinated seeds.

Plant cells expand upward through the process of geotropism.

Lights out—photosynthesis occurs.

Bees feed their offspring from pollinated flowers.

Birds engineer the dispersant of seeds.

Perched on the tree branch, they sing a tune to wake us up.

We fly out of bed to start the day.

Perfume vigorously sprayed to suffocate the room.

The smell of coffee beans makes us fully conscious.

The taste of yogurt parfait enjoyed before we head out.

Pets hurriedly given a kiss goodbye.

The day has begun and the cycle repeats.

Airplanes

Over the plains there's a chicken coop.

A loud sound from nearby frightens the flock.

I look up at the sky with large eyes of admiration.

There it is.

A white streak that grows bigger with every mile reached.

Its body descending rapidly through the hoary clouds.

Wings slope downward; it appears to be vertical now.

Cycling through the firmament, it misses the coop by a few inches.

Thousands of miles from home; the plane soon finds its landing.

I gather the group and head back inside.

Spiked-Stars

The air is crisp and clean.

We're no longer surrounded by polluted forces.

There's been an uptick of recycling; we can finally breathe.

Ice caps are now slow to melt.

Greenhouse gases are at bay; the sun has reduced its glare.

I go outside to the top of the hill.

Before me lies millions of stars.

I gaze at each one of them, careful not to undermine their magnitude.

Jagged gamma rays form flawless imaging.

Velvet glow burns brightly.

Constant illusions of where the Earth stands.

Starry eyes of the natural sight.

SECTION 2

Grounded in Society

Suffering & Smiling

Grinds & Flows

Hard work valued above all else.

But hard work alone won't make you successful.

I think it takes a bit of prayer and luck to keep the momentum going.

Hypercompetitive mindset to build up a society.

Sweat stains on our clothes—whatever it takes.

Bills paid, children fed, what else is left over?

They say work hard and play harder, but I'm not fond of games.

Disposable income unanchored in the industrialized system.

Common influences of authority figures.

There's a profound effect.

Struggles We Face

Humans learn how to spend and consume.

But most struggle to save.

How can you really save when you've got expenses that need to be paid?

We count all our dollars, but still, it's not enough.

Though, we try to make our money count.

Even if it's for the short run.

Rules and boundaries are defied.

Broken systems erase documentations.

Authority from within; there's much pressure from society.

We're told that more education leads to success.

But what was so different with the anomalies?

Realisms

Out of touch with the realities of society.

Management of emotions just to keep up with the task at hand.

We're in too deep.

Point of view changed once life comes at us quickly.

Day jobs warrant ordinary stress.

Feeling small, we're just another number.

Ironic worries.

Isolated even though we're surrounded by other people.

Stuck in a gloom, what's the outcome?

The hope is that someday things will become easier.

Competition

Vultures pulled down from climbing to the top.

Exploitation of their grueling nature.

It's getting down to the wire.

We try to stick out in the crowded room.

Walls built to separate the haves from the have nots.

They can't see the end of the road.

The battle lies ahead; we're being tested every day.

Control-stained prisms, we continue to cast blame.

Working overtime to make ends meet.

There's a linger of overcompensation.

But true freedom comes from within.

Still Looking, Still Dreaming

Thoughts of failure and regret consume my mind.

Education obtained to make more money.

But where is the money?

Careful decisions made to not spend too much.

Shortage of jobs, working harder isn't the answer.

I haven't slept in a while.

It doesn't feel like I have my whole life ahead of me.

Pastel nights, teardrops stain my pillowcase.

Tongue tied interviews; I can already predict the outcome.

Unspoken words, but I gave them my authentic self.

It just wasn't meant to be.

Comfort and easement soon overtake.

I won't allow myself to give up.

Though I suffer in silence, my outward appearance tells a different story.

Suffering & Smiling

I can't stop dreaming.

I can't stop working.

Labels shredded into pieces, for I am able.

It isn't over.

Grit

Suffocating in the thick of it.

We seek to live a better life.

The weight of our worries brought back down to Earth.

The past has now faded; we take hold of our future.

Open and free, we make our own path.

We won't give up.

Heels dug deeply into the dirt.

Knees scraped from playing with the pavement.

We call out from below when we start to lose control.

Shadows casted out from the gleaming light.

'til we make it, we will continue to fake it.

Newfound Changes

Doubters cannot believe their eyes.

They said I'd never make it.

But no one sees the hard work you put in.

They would rather choose to focus on the fruits of your labor.

"Wow, you are so lucky!"

Instant gratification.

But I've waited my whole life for this moment.

Years of mental collisions.

All I had were my dreams.

Still, I know success can vanish in a minute.

So, I remain grateful for all my accomplishments.

Familial Connections

Hearty Questions

Can you still be sufficient and have trauma?

Are abusive tendencies genetic or a result of your environment?

Will we ever be content?

Does your upbringing determine your future?

Can we ever completely heal?

Are we alone in our thoughts?

The Figurine

Dressed up to perfection with a smile on my face.

Beauty is pain, now stand still.

Decorated ornament to show off to the world.

Lipstick wiped away to reveal the truth.

Doses of medicine leave a bitter tang.

Impressions illustrated to portray an image.

Depictions of a life not ever lived.

Silicone sippy cups rot the intestines.

Communal backings once unraveled.

Tormented by the insecurities, we remain hopeless.

Breaking Free

Robbed of my formative years.

Flesh and blood plagued my youth.

Memories of the mishandling.

Wounded in fetal position.

Misused like a toy.

The walls of my world caved in.

Innocent child turned cold.

Five. Seven. Twelve. Fourteen.

Frustration of the silent screams.

Tortured by the pressures of society.

The storm rising inside of me grew in agony.

The Never-ending Race

Dysfunctional family crocheted the welted scars.

Expectations often found unachievable.

The homeostasis of the group stood firm and tall.

Who was going to be the prodigy?

Nonsensical comparisons created division.

Unwrapped pride flew past the parcel.

Loveless life found around the lock.

Nothing ever came easy.

One day you'll come back down to Earth.

Character Built

Protecting myself from the blows of the night.

Chills and sweats wash over me.

The days repeat with no end in sight.

Words seamlessly pruned to perfection.

Picturesque troubles completed by the overflow.

Naps throughout the day to forget about reality.

Dreams about an alternate life.

Out of touch, I'm awoken again.

Ideas and fears drawn out with tears.

It's no big deal.

Friend to Myself

I've always been taught to follow my heart.

Practical degrees with a touch of passion.

Self-fulfilling prophecy, I've found my peace.

Mended relationships: I was silent all along.

Fine on the outside, that's the only thing that mattered.

Pretending with a heavy heart.

Falling apart, to pieces I returned.

Friend to myself, I can truly rely on.

Rooted

Touch deprived, it sometimes sucks to be lonely.

Therapy to heal from past traumas.

Medical treatments to repair my brain.

Inside my home there will be understanding.

Seeds planted will arise at the crack of dawn.

I'll lay down the roots of the wooden foundation.

A place where my children can roam freely without a care in the world.

Unwelcomed guests will vanish from my castle's walls.

By the windowsills, I'll write about whatever comes to mind.

The winds of the world can no longer knock me down.

For I am a force to be reckon with.

SECTION 3

Grounded in Self

Body Inhibitions

Fluticasone Lungs

My organ seeks to float on inorganic compounds.

Air-filled alveoli, oxygen is needed.

Windpipes knocked down; cilia can't filter this one out.

The walls of the trachea are quickly closing in on me.

Foreign particles have made its way into the bronchi.

Dehydrated exercises cause unwanted inducements.

Narrow esophagus, bite-sized pieces are recommended.

Airways inflamed, it's now hard to breathe.

I'm taking shorter breaths, realizing how I've taken the act of breathing for granted.

I cough and wheeze, praying that this won't be my last inhale.

Chronic disease, how many are affected?

Steroid inhalers won't work, I need a rescue one.

Body Inhibitions

Tightness in the chest, I don't want a ventilator.

Trying to fix it on my own, but I know I need help.

Thought it was finally gone, but this is a lifelong development.

Now left with an intercostal muscle strain, I wallow in pain.

Aching Arthritis

My arms and hands rest in a stiff-like position.

It's because of all the medicine I've taken.

Essentially, I'm flawed.

Opening and carrying things bring me great aches.

Inflamed joints grow with redness.

Fluid rush to the palm of my hands.

It's warm to the touch.

The wear and tear of my labor have grown upon me.

Yoga helps a bit unless I go a few days without it.

Unknown cause, I'm too young to go through this.

Another day, another flare-up.

Nobody knows the pain I go through.

Invisible illness, I was once free.

Joints buckle and bolt, my rheumatologist says to take steroids.

No cure, we want to enter the remissive phase.

Pain reduced; I hope to one day delay decay.

Purging

I do not binge.

So, it doesn't make sense.

Tummy full of food, fluids must now be excreted.

My second toothbrush always seems to get the job done.

Acid reflux, my stomach has never been the same.

I have a need to want to control my life.

So, I only eat once a day.

Numbers on the scale always tell me lies.

Distorted body image, I never know what to believe.

Comorbidities, my brain has been through enough.

Aren't you tired yet?

I know that I am.

Dysmorphic Tales

My body is upset with me.

I have betrayed and let it go.

Lightning strikes, cellulite remains.

Stomach starts to bulge.

Why am I always bloated?

Thin, plump, solid flabs.

Layers of blubber lie under the skin.

Adipose tissue consumes the buttery oils.

I can't get rid of it.

Stuck, my body has betrayed me.

Gained weight moves and grooves to the sound of my cries.

Ashamed with the defects, I cover up my flaws.

The mirrors still know me by name.

Are they really distorted?

Hives

I am a child of nature.

Grass and trees cause asthmatic flare-ups.

Walks around the reservoir quickly become dangerous.

Tingling sensation on my skin means trouble lies nearby.

Body overreacts to pressure from the ecosystem.

The irritants find its way through my layers of clothing.

Skin welts form from the allergic reaction.

I start to itch.

Continuous massage to exert force onto my body.

Chronic beginnings, it lasts for 45 minutes at a time.

Areata

---

7 years of pain and longing.

Haven't I suffered enough?

Gray areas met with patchiness of the scalp.

Immune system fought fervently on my behalf.

But it was the wrong enemy.

My body fought with itself.

Great stress led to thinner follicles.

Cortisone shots pierced through my skin.

I silently wept.

Slowly, I learned to love myself from within.

For if someone is ever to truly love me, they must first understand me deeply.

Monumental beauty displayed for the world to ostracize.

I was made stronger.

Gaping Black Hole

Misfired neurons, my thoughts are not my own.

Disassociation findings, I cannot make decisions.

Drowning in unchanged debt, why did I spend so much?

But we were meant to be together.

For he is my soulmate.

Uncomfortable delusions.

Reality no longer exists.

Passive ideation, I successfully manage.

Episodes run from the sound of stability.

I can't just snap out of it.

Static motions to reduce the stigma.

I hope one day you'll understand my truth.

SECTION 4

Grounded in Humanity

City Life?

Peoplehood

Nationality, ethnicity, and culture help to define you.

We're made consciously aware of our physical characteristics.

Prejudicial attitudes rooted in hostility and hatred.

We face discrimination and disadvantages.

Cities change with the help of technology.

Artificial intelligence leads to the formation of self-driven cars.

Industrial economies cause population movements.

Millions of people; cities are growing.

Persecution and war incentivize people to seek asylum.

Changes in government, where is it ever safe?

Climate change creates urban redesign.

Fluid gridlines: the neighborhood is organized differently.

Pedestrians want to improve their quality of life.

But so many buildings are left vacant and unused.

City Life?

The flow of money and entertainment continue to drive cities.

Tourism is a work of art like museums.

Revolutionize spaces to encourage social activism.

We've been promised to have a world of stability.

Print + Digital Culture

Audience members consume art and music through their everyday activities.

Private spaces now filled with chatter of politics.

Sponsors of entertainment form new social classes.

Opinions expressed through the help of the internet.

Impressionable minds lack the skill of discernment.

Arenas of sociability we start to hang out in.

Public opinions formed to learn about new phenomenon.

Embodied enlightenment to promote interactions.

But reason finds its way missing from civil discourses.

The arbiter of truth substituted for relentless name-calling.

The marketplace of ideas has become immune to criticism.

Every voice matters, but rarely do we ever speak.

Stimulated energy from the commercial exchanges.

Wasted platforms continue to do no good.

Delisted membership to see a promulgated change.

Snapshot Friendship

70-year age gap, how can this be?

4-hour train ride from Venice to Vienna, my eyes gazed out into the open land.

Silver snow covered the mountain hills.

The sun pierced through my dark brown eyes.

In Innsbruck, a calm voice asked to sit down next to me.

But I wanted to be alone in my adoration.

Little did I know that one conversation would turn into a 7-year-long friendship.

Born in a different time, where B-17 bombs would rapidly land feet away from him.

There was no choosing which side you'd belong to.

Child soldiers made to serve as spies.

This wasn't a fair way of living.

Hiding in the forest until the war was over.

There would be no free ticket to the land of opportunity.

City Life?

Blueberry pickings from the bushes; oh, don't you dare walk close to the border line.

Arrested and sent to jail, justice was never sought.

No security checkpoints in present day, what a privilege it is to live in the free world.

General surgeon by day, mountaineer come sundown.

There's no stopping my old friend.

Multiple perspectives found, do we ever really learn from our mistakes?

Decisions made that we're not proud of; we can only seek to do better.

Sense of Fear

I walked along the sidewalk of this city with a sense of fear.

Fearful that this group would attack me for the color of my skin.

Fearful that another ethnic group had continued to be persecuted and ostracized there.

Fearful at the fact that this group boldly made their presence known.

Hm, what was the image on that individual's sweatshirt?

Oh yeah, we don't talk about it, she said to me.

Public displays of their emotions, they never live in fear.

Their government does little to stop the racism there.

Democracy and equality sing a different tune.

Animalistic drawings on posters to depict an image.

A similar thing happened not too far from my hometown.

Different places, but similar ideologies.

Some are afraid of diversity.

Fear breeds hatred.

What is the fate of humanity?

Identity

We came into the world with a name, a source of identity.

But many died having that identity tormented.

Names stripped, replaced with a number.

Some given Western names to "assimilate" better.

Both groups unvarnished of their pride and dignity.

Both got on their knees to scrub the concrete streets.

Both continuously told that they are the reason of their country's failure.

Both told and treated as though they were underserving of life.

Unfathomable exchanges.

But why do we choose to remember and mourn one group's experience over the other?

Weren't both experiences detrimental to our understanding of history?

Is one group simply more palatable because of the color of their skin?

Both should be remembered.

City Life?

Both deserve monuments and museums.

Both histories deserve to be taught in our classes so that we may never forget the harm done.

There can be no absolvent when those in the past played such an active role.

You cannot expect to have a trust of authority if those in power refuse to reconcile with their painful history.

The descendants of both groups continue to exist and hurt.

We know who was affected, somewhat understand how it happened, but fail to remember it.

Untold Story

Eyes stare at me eager to converse.

Uncomfortable feeling, my other conversation came to an abrupt end.

Thick accent and stutter, I struggle to make out his words.

Gestures created through the movement of hands.

From Turkey to Hungary, he sought refuge.

Persecuted for his choice of religion, there were no opportunities left.

Safety over economic advantage is what he truly desired.

17-year-old boy faced with much hardship.

It's one thing to hear the numbers, and another to listen to individual stories.

History will never truly stay in the past, for there will always be eye-witness accounts.

It is an ongoing process that helps guide our future.

Cultivated Crisis

With very little energy left, I found myself hungry.

I entered a fast-food chain looking for something good.

An enthusiastic woman jumped in while I was conversing with the cashier.

She followed me to my seat; I could tell she had a lot on her mind.

I asked her if she would like to join me for lunch, to which she said yes.

We conversed for over an hour.

From Pakistan to Denmark, she's been in Europe since she was two.

This 50-year-old woman told me that she's still treated as a foreigner there.

As a child, she gleefully played with the other friendly children.

She once felt like a true Dane.

To her, nationality has little to do with blood.

But everything to do with citizenship and assimilation.

City Life?

People often stare at her family and make quick judgments.

They tell her that there are no jobs left in the country because of her "kind of people."

The citizens fear for their safety, but this lady fears for her safety as well.

She's having an identity crisis.

For many, it can look like choosing your wants and desires.

But for her, it is a matter of belonging and security.

Some people are afraid to support her business and decide to bully her.

She is proud to be a Dane, but also wants Danes to see her as an equal.

Integration and assimilation are sometimes not enough.

Treated differently despite being fluent in the native tongue.

It doesn't matter all your accolades.

You will always be seen as a foreigner.

Economic
Restorations

Hand Ups

Rapidly growing markets, executive skills are needed.

Unwanted field of dreams.

Scarce resources create compromised opportunities.

Vulnerable shortages, there's a heightened awareness.

Context changes, your purpose is defined.

Loans paid off with modest amounts of money.

Dignity restored.

Increased demand drives competitive sales.

Reliable nature searches for safety nets.

Material comfort creates interdependent chaos.

Fractured governments unite to formulate the agenda.

Luck of the draw, it's not easy to climb out of poverty.

Globalization becomes hostile to new entrants.

Economic Restorations

Fixable change, there's been no growth.

Still, we rely on neighbors for their natural resources.

Countries that missed the boat are often condemned.

When will they see prosperity?

Global Phenomenon

Goods trade at the flow of capital.

We visualize a migration of people.

Each so distinct, they're from a different dimension.

Raw materials exported, our GDP increases.

Commodities never fail to generate income inequality.

But what are we left with?

Rapid developments value labor over land.

Infinite possibilities lead to expansion.

Jobs created; wages multiply, the market tightens up just a bit.

Trade alone will not help those at the bottom.

Export diversification, traps get unlocked.

We rely on natural resources in land-locked countries.

But some developing nations can be rescued from within.

The Nethermost Billion

Quick to find solutions, we find ourselves stuck.

Each time we fail to identify the problem.

How did this happen?

Missed pinpoints, we search for answers.

Still, they cannot escape.

Some make less than one dollar a day.

They grow with righteous frustration.

Shouldn't everyone have the chance to participate in globalism?

Executed ideas detect possible shortcomings.

Quiet minds learn to first understand.

Confident incentives, they soon make effective decisions.

We give them the reins to control their future.

It was no happenstance.

Empowered people learn to innovate.

Ideologies align with their culture and traditions.

Economic Restorations

They learn how to sustain themselves.

Efficient outcomes are produced.

Confidence is restored.

This is justice.

Sink and Swim

Venice is sinking.

9 inches, its land has seen great flooding.

Industries gleefully participate in fracking.

They carelessly dig out underwater channels.

Maritime goals ruined by sea water's gush.

Surges of high storms, the water flows over banks of sea.

Mud flats aid by cushioning against the water.

Drained up land for airports to be created.

Why are the buildings resting on wooden pillars?

The Mediterranean can no longer shield against the lagoon.

Overpopulation of people, some have decided to leave.

Human activity continues to warm the planet.

Is there enough energy to go around?

The Agreement

Global Era sees expansion of foreign investment.

There's a search for the source of capital.

Barriers to trade are removed.

Speculation rises to a second degree.

Dire consequences on developed nations.

Have they truly contributed?

Investors are zealously protected.

Host countries are left to fend for themselves.

They lack the resources to grow and develop.

Forceful control of both people and land.

Many are left feeling exposed and exploited.

Unbalanced power dynamics, they ignore the terms of the agreement.

Unsighted signatures, they hope for a better future.

Economic Restorations

Once withdrawn, nations are filled with a sense of emptiness.

Weariness is what they know.

Suspicion once turned into rejection, they now welcome with open arms.

Was there ever a grand bargain?

Free-Rider

The focus is on the people.

They are encouraged to be resilient and consistent.

The government provides insurance in case of an emergency.

Sufficient amounts of money, we have a good plan.

Resources allocated to enhance welfare.

But it's at the expense of another.

We aim to be in a place of neutrality.

Where no one is made worse off and at least one person's status improves.

Economic mobility.

The distribution pie increases its size.

We list the criteria to help diminish poverty.

Optimal standards made on efficiency grounds.

Wealth maximization thrives on utility.

Well-informed individuals find desirable transactions.

Developed Leadership

You must always listen to me.

For I am your boss.

I have the knowledge to hold you accountable.

Words of affirmation from compliant requests.

You follow my direction.

Submission to authority, my wish is your command.

For you are now accepted by me.

But this is no way to live, Sir.

I urge you to come to me as you are.

I won't define you by your past.

Loved beyond measure, you have always been valuable.

Willingly you follow, I never demand.

Doubts casted out, we work as a team.

Harmonious life, rapport is built.

Lessons Learned

The Neighbor

To lay alongside your neighbor in times of need is to love.

But the people nearby me come crumbling down.

As they step away, I start to step up.

Step up to help those who cannot help themselves.

Attitudes change; we have a new opportunity.

Natural inclinations, we sacrifice convenience.

Comforted by our actions, we start to stretch.

For this life is bigger than you and me.

Barriers break down to build new bridges.

Intentional relations, our walls get strengthened.

Callous foes mistreat questionable subordinates.

They hide behind their fears and shame.

They use cruel words to maim and cut others deeply.

Lessons Learned

But we're moved by the act of healing.

We absorb the costs of restoration.

Our souls learn to maintain peace.

For time is of the essence.

Forgiven Freedom

I counted your faults and all that you owed me.

For a long time, I resented you deeply.

You hurt, rejected, abandoned, and betrayed me.

Experiences that too many people can relate to.

My mind blocked out the painful memories.

But sometimes they still come creeping back up to my conscious.

Payback and grudges were nurtured in my soul.

Revenge was seemingly justified.

Though it is in my nature to forgive.

Oh, how difficult of a task it has proven to be.

An ongoing process, I no longer keep count of your offenses.

I extend forgiveness to you because without love, I am nothing.

Decisions made; compassion is what I choose.

A newfound joy, we choose to celebrate.

For there's an opportunity to show grace.

Lessons Learned

Withholding forgiveness brought bondage to my heart.

Anger and guilt ate away at my essence.

Spiritual oppression, I was being devoured.

Psychosomatic; there was an internal conflict.

Forgiveness never feels fair.

But alas, I let go.

Opaque Findings

Where are you lost?

Butterflies visualized through human eyes.

There's a defenseless separation.

Combination of stories, we were once lost.

Heretofore, we made rash decisions.

Welcomed into the world, there's been an awakening.

Wandering away, it's a bad investment.

Crisis! Crisis!

This moment in life is paused.

But we can recover.

We're given back what was once taken.

Responsibility accepted; we go forward in life.

Coming to our senses, we seek to change.

Celebrations from rejoiced new comings.

Lessons Learned

But foes don't want to see you get better.

Courtside jealousy, there's a lack of excitement.

Bitter resentment, I do not shake.

Oh, how I wish it could be different.

Blind Spots

Tender hearts are clothed with love.

Serene peace flows through our hearts.

We get along in the ongoing process.

Drained personas: I seek to be healthier.

Common denominator, I may be the issue.

Changes made, there's a sense of self-control.

Blind spots we refuse to look at.

What are the faults in your own life?

Inward developments, it's time to breathe and release.

New transformations made, we become more experienced.

Dedications to consistency; reflections take place.

Dumped out emotions, where is our healing?

Yielding to the fullness of our lives.

Lessons Learned

Burdens we begin to let go of.

Composed weariness, the present is slippery.

Our determined future is currently elusive.

Prefatory engagements: I want to start over.

The Eyes

In this realm, I am continuously learning.

Expressions I trust, will it ever be enough?

Malignant hearts fail to question how big their hearts are.

It's the principle.

Limited resources, this is your capability.

Fair access into my mind, I am deeply known.

Judgmental eyes watch over me.

They say I haven't given enough.

But this is all I have to offer.

True generosity is never demanded.

Scaled to perfection, there's no reluctance from me.

Kind eyes look over me with curiosity.

They see that my heart is in the right place.

Treasures lie along green pastures.

Released human tendencies; I start to develop.

Lessons Learned

Prosperous spirits—material possessions have no hold on me.

Greed and fear are banished from my world.

Advancements made to create a new society.

We continue to gain and will win in the end.

Joyful bliss remains.

Shapeable Perseverance

Disheartened, disappointed, yet we continue to defy.

Patient hearts soon discover the plan.

Voices of reason listen ardently.

Pay attention to the subtle moments of silence.

Non-negotiable determinations, we enter a new direction.

Perfect guidance quakes at the sound of expectancy.

Perspective limited; we thirst for wisdom.

Tuned in convictions are made corrected.

Encouraged to do better; I fervently participate.

Eye floaters rubbed away.

Clearer sights to discover my calling.

Commitments made; I don't want to disappoint.

Haughty foes want me to be unfocused.

But I resist their fulsome pleasantries.

Cromulent responses, I know who to follow.

Lessons Learned

Willingness to change; I now seek pure pleasures.

Painted observations, there's no wavering obligation.

Backed-up actions, we start to follow through with our words.

Completion sowed into our hearts.

For we are now rooted.

Clothed in Love

Love once limited by issues that were hindered.

Casted out projections, we have a tendency to judge.

Bright-lined assumptions, we're still hurting from our wounds.

Filtered relationships, who can we truly relate to?

Inward healing to love more broadly.

Instructions designed; we start to follow the command.

Respected dynamics, we learn how to fully love.

People we write off and deem unlovable.

Though they need it the most.

The lost will soon find their refuge.

But what is our responsibility?

Put into practice, we take some steps forward.

Complex reactions; there's a new demonstration.

Risked connections fulfilled through shared assistance.

Take cover in sacrificial agape.

CPSIA information can be obtained
at www.ICGtesting.com
Printed in the USA
BVHW041013040523
663596BV00003B/38

9 781665 743129